Losing Someone You Love

Losing Someone
You Love

◆

When a Brother or Sister Dies

TEXT AND PHOTOGRAPHS BY

Elizabeth Richter

G. P. PUTNAM'S SONS

New York

Library of Congress Cataloging in Publication Data
Richter, Elizabeth. Losing someone you love.
Summary: Sixteen young people ranging in age from ten to
twenty-four describe the fears, sorrow, and other emotions
they experienced when a brother or sister died.
1. Death—Psychological aspects—United States—
Case studies—Juvenile literature. 2. Death—
Social aspects—United States—Case Studies—
Juvenile literature. 3. Brothers and sisters—
United States—Case studies—Juvenile literature.
4. Bereavement—Psychological aspects—Case studies—
Juvenile literature. [1. Death. 2. Brothers and sisters]
I. Title
HQ1073.3.R53   1986   155.9'37   85-12395
ISBN 0-399-21243-4

*This book is dedicated to
my brother Barry Richter
and to the Popp Family,
in memory of Connie*

✦

*and to my friends
the McGrade Family*

Contents

✦

Introduction

✦

Several months ago I went to the funeral of a young woman, who was close to my family. Because of the interviewing I had done for this book, talking with many young people who were coping with the death of a brother or sister, I believed I had learned something very important. Every one of the kids I spoke with wanted to talk about what he or she was feeling. But though I had learned this lesson through the work on my book, I still failed to use what I learned in a crisis situation nearest to me.

After the funeral, when family and friends gathered at the parents' home, I found myself doing just what other adults often do when talking to young surviving siblings. I vividly remember asking Kathleen, the young woman's fourteen-year-old sister, "How is school this year?" After searching for an answer, she said, "I don't really want to talk about school right now." I would not have asked her mother or father, "How is your job?" at such a time. Why would I ask Kathleen about school?

Despite all the hugs and kisses and thanks I received from kids I listened to for the book, I didn't give Kathleen what she needed. I asked myself why I missed the boat with her, and came to the conclusion that when this kind of crisis hits close to home, many of us, even the most sensitive and knowledgeable, make mistakes. But, as adults—parents, family, friends and professionals—we need to persist in opening lines of communication for our children, difficult as that may be. The most obvious need expressed by all the young people I spoke with was a desperate desire to be heard and for their feelings to be accepted, not judged, not ignored. Their questions did not always require answers, but they longed for compassion and understanding.

It is my hope that the interviews in this book reach the hearts of other young people who have lost a brother or sister and who are feeling hurt and confused. I think the sharing of experiences always helps us to feel less isolated and may give some the courage to reach out for a helping hand, inside or outside the home.

Some months after I interviewed eighteen-year-old Lisa for this book, I received a letter from her. She wanted to share with me something she had written in school. Her assignment had been to describe something that had changed her life, and she chose to write about my interview with her. Here is part of what Lisa wrote:

> When I first started I had so many feelings that made me very confused, but since Elizabeth was so understanding we took it slow. I explained to her how it happened and, the hardest thing of all, I told her how everything made me feel. A little while went by, and when I looked at Elizabeth she looked very sad. I didn't want to see her upset, but it made me feel good knowing that someone I had just met was so sensitive toward me and everything that had happened. I finally shared the pain and anger I felt and still feel today.

After talking to Elizabeth about my problem she told me about some of the other teenagers she had interviewed. This helped me, knowing that I wasn't alone, but I also feel hurt for them because I had been through what they were going through, losing someone you love. One more thing that made me feel good was knowing that some day someone will pick up the book and read my story, and it may help someone like Elizabeth has helped me.

Each family that participated in the making of this book expressed clearly their desire to help other children and parents through this lonely crisis. It was not an easy decision that the parents made in granting me permission to let their children speak, nor was it easy for the children to open up to a stranger, expressing their deepest feelings. But I was reassured after each interview, by both the young people and their parents, of the need for this book. It was confirmed over and over again that sisters and brothers want their pain recognized, that sibling grief, different as it is from parental grief, hurts and needs our serious and loving attention.

—Elizabeth Richter

Bitsy

✦

AGE 17

Her twin sister Ann and their best friend
Katie were killed in a head-on collision.

The accident happened on a Friday night in July six months ago. School was out and we weren't working. I didn't have plans that night and I wanted to go out with Ann and Katie, our friend, but Ann and I got into a fight and she walked out. I was angry because she left without me.

That night I had trouble sleeping. I've always known when something was wrong with Ann. My older sister Amy came to the door of my bedroom, and she was shaking. She told me there'd been an accident. We went to the hospital, and I kept saying, "It's all my fault because we had a fight."

It was just getting light when we reached the hospital. Ann was in surgery. At first the doctor told us Ann was blind, and then that she had brain damage. I went out to talk to Larry, my boyfriend, and I heard my mom scream. I ran in, and she said, "Annie died." I went running through the halls, screaming. Then we were told about Katie.

We called my big brother Phil, and he came home from school. He looked sick and he'd been crying. It was not the Phil I had ever seen before. I looked up to him like a father. It was weird seeing that he had been crying.

My relationship to my brother and sister is different from mine with Ann. It's nothing like being a twin and it doesn't help me get over Ann. Six months after the accident it's still *our* room, *our* car. I've never had anything that's mine, it was always ours. We always shared our clothes. It's weird going to bed with an empty bed next to mine. When a friend is sleeping over, in the night I turn over and see the figure and think it's Ann. Then I realize it's not.

I'm trying so hard to remember her voice, and it's scary to think of that going away. The hardest part for me is that I know I'm not going to be growing up with Ann. I won't have her to share my life with. I won't have her at my graduation with me or as a maid of honor. It's scary. I can't imagine telling people when I'm forty that I had a sister and she died when she was seventeen. And that's the way it's going to be at college. No one will know about us.

Reality doesn't set in for so long. It still hasn't for me. I want this stage to be over with, but the process seems a million miles away. I keep wanting to be vulnerable but I think it's not even me who wants to hurt more, it's other people.

People have expectations for me. The first week it was all eyes on Bitsy, the girl who lost her twin sister. I remember I went to a party and people were whispering behind my back, "Why is she here? She should be at home, wearing black." Then after two weeks they think you should be on top of the world and they wonder why I cry at school, like on anniversaries, when it's the seventeenth of the month. That's difficult, a dreaded D-Day. Or at something someone says that reminds me of her, or like today I looked at my fingernails and they looked like hers. There are days when I look in the mirror and I get choked.

I don't want the white-glove treatment. I'm not fragile but I don't want to be treated as though it never happened. There has got to be a middle point. Friends should try not to make judgments, like "Why isn't she upset?" or "Why is she?"

The worst thing is to push away the living. My mom used to take down the pictures of the two of us. She idolized Ann. I always felt that Ann was the good one and I was the bad one. I don't want to be jealous of Ann now that she's dead. I felt that way when she was alive, but I don't want to feel that way now. I know that deep down inside, my mom is not sorry that it was Ann instead of me, but sometimes I feel that way. Sometimes I think I feel guilty for surviving.

Larry

♦

AGE 18

*Larry is Bitsy's boyfriend. His brother Jason,
age seven, was hit by a car while he was playing
at the side of the road. The driver had been
working all night and fell asleep at the wheel.*

I was thirteen and I was in junior high. I was in my math class
when I got a message to go to the office. The rabbi was there
and he said there had been an accident. I thought it was my
mom, but he said, "No, it's your brother," and he told me my
brother was dead. He drove me to the hospital.

When I went back to school, I felt so alien. I felt as though
everyone was watching me. It was bad at the time, but now I
see they were just concerned and wondered what they could do
to help.

I still can't talk to my dad about it. My parents are more
protective of me since the accident. I understand this, but it
bothers me.

Bitsy used to tell me I should talk about it. One time she kept
bugging me to talk, bugging me to go to the cemetery, bugging
me to cry. I blew up at her. "What do you think you are, a
psychologist?"

What happened to Ann did stir up old feelings, but it helped
me to see Bitsy go through it. I could understand more about
what I was going through, and it made me realize that I could
help her. I told her that it was going to hurt for a while but that
in a few years she'd be able to look back and have really good
memories about Ann. You're not going to spend your whole life
having nightmares and crying. There is something to look forward to.

Marc

✦

AGE 13

His baby brother died of crib death
(Sudden Infant Death Syndrome).

Crib death is when babies die in their sleep, and doctors really don't know why. I was only four when my little brother Joseph died, but when I look at pictures I can remember him. I also remember specific events.

We woke up in the morning, and my mom and I walked into the room where my brother was. She went over to his crib and touched him, and the next thing I remember she was running outside to get the neighbors. Then the police came and they took my mom. I went with them.

When Joseph first died, my mom acted like she was in space. She didn't talk to me for a while, and I heard her cry. I never saw my dad cry, not once. I remember my mom sitting up at night. She was really worried, and she didn't get enough sleep. Sometimes she would get mad for no reason, but then she'd say, "Excuse me, Marc, I didn't mean what I said. I'm just tired. I didn't sleep well last night."

When Michael was born, I thought the same thing was going to happen to him for a while there. I thought he was going to leave just like Joseph did. Then, when I turned nine, my mom explained that crib death only happens during certain ages, and after that you don't have to worry about it.

I got kind of jealous with her watching Michael all the time. You remember things like that. It wasn't until recently that I got over being jealous of my little brother.

If someone went away, I always felt they wouldn't come back. I was afraid my mom would go away to work and never come home. "Are you going to disappear just like my brother did?" I remember asking.

It would have helped when I was little if they'd told me that no one else is ever going to leave, but then that wouldn't have been true. If you're little and something happens, it's kind of scary. It's a big deal and that's what makes you remember it so much.

It's very important, my mom being honest. I can talk to her about anything. If she had told me a lot of stuff that wasn't true, then I think it would have hurt me a lot.

I think I value life more than most kids my age. I understand a little more about what's important.

Vicky

♦

AGE 17

Her brother Freddy, age 19, was killed
when his moped was hit by a truck in Mexico.

On his birth certificate my brother's name was Frederick Field
Stevens IV, but people called him Fred, and since I was little I
called him Freddy. He was nineteen, four years older than me,
and a fantastic artist and an extraordinary person, who was into
astronomy, philosophy, everything.

We'd gone down to Cozumel, which is an island off the
Yucatan Peninsula in Mexico, for a family vacation. We'd been
there before, when I was small, and my brother had been there
for two summers to stay with the Zapata family and worked on
a scuba-diving boat.

That day, Monday, had been really nice. My brother and
father were scuba diving, and my mother and I were snorkeling
above them. We were all exhausted when we went back to the
hotel, but my brother decided to go over on his rented moped
to see Ramon, the father of the family who owned the scuba-
diving boat he'd worked on. A few seconds after he left, he
came back and said he didn't want to take the picture of Ramon

he'd been planning to carry because it was so windy that the picture might be ruined. I guess we should have realized then how windy it was for the moped.

My mother and I were so tired we took a nap. Suddenly we heard my father pounding on the door, saying my brother had been in an accident. He had been hit by a truck.

We were taken over to the hospital in a sort of van. I ran in ahead of my parents, but no one spoke English. When my parents came in, my mom was taken into a room and all of a sudden we heard her scream. My dad and I just grabbed each other, and we knew what had happened.

I don't even remember how we got back to the hotel, though we must have been taken back in the van. We were sitting in the lobby, which was kind of tropical, when the Zapatas came in. It had been so long since I had seen them, but they were just like our family. They kissed and hugged us because they had heard about Freddy.

I don't really remember too much about what happened next. I know we were brought down to the police station the next day, to file an accident report and other technical stuff. I just looked down. Even when we went to the cemetery to see the plot, I looked down. I held on to someone, whoever was there. My feelings were all kind of scrambled up. I was walking around like a zombie.

Wednesday was the funeral. The girls from the Zapata family went out and picked wildflowers. It was so nice. I don't know what we would have done if it hadn't been for them. First we went to a church and we sat there for hours, just crying and thinking about it. I glanced up and the casket was there, but I couldn't look at it. I remember staring at these blinking lights in the church, like Christmas lights, so that I wouldn't have to look at the casket. When we walked out, I just stared at the ground. We were there in this huge courtyard, like a kind of park, and we walked there for a really long time.

Then my mother and I were put in a station wagon, and when we turned around, we saw my brother's casket was in the back. We drove very slowly because all these people were walking behind the car. I guess they knew my brother from when he was there before. We reached the graveyard and got out, but I just stared at the ground and held on to someone. I had to be led around like a blind person.

Everything was in Spanish. First of all they said a Hail Mary for each rosary bead. By the end I was just saying it along with them, not knowing what it was. I don't think I can even say it in English.

Finally the crypt belonging to the Zapatas was opened up. It's above the ground because of being on an island. They'd wanted Freddy to be in their family burial place. I saw Ramon take a flower to put in the casket, and I noticed that my brother was wearing the shirt I had given him for Christmas. The thing that hurt a lot was watching them seal the crypt with cement when they put the door on.

We went home that night. We had to change planes in Florida, and we nearly missed our flight because we hadn't adjusted our watches for the time change. When we got home, I think I was the first one in the house, and it was really cold and morbid-looking and empty. Everything was going on around me. One of the first things my parents did was to call people to tell them what had happened. And I remember hearing and hearing my mom and father talking, my mother crying. It was just horrible.

My brother and I shared a bathroom, so now whenever I'm in there, I feel so lonely. I think about the times we were fooling around and he'd throw cold water on me. At night, I don't know what it is, but I have to have his door closed and my door closed. It's not like when we were kids and used to have the doors open, talking back and forth to each other.

Lately I've been wanting my family to get closer, but it's not working. I think I'm trying. It seems like it's two against one in our house now. I guess every child wants to impress his or her parents, but now it seems I want to try harder. I just want them to accept me as me. I feel I'm sort of like a possession that

they're saving. It's like if you have two valuable coins and you lose one, you hold onto the other one tighter. That's the way I feel, like I've got to be careful because if anything happens to me it will kill them.

My brother's best friend Clifton came to visit once with his family. We were up in my brother's room, and Clifton was talking about him, and he just started crying. It was the first time that I talked to someone who knew my brother like I knew him, and it was the first time that somebody could understand my feelings. My eyes were just welling up. I respect the fact that Clifton could cry because I hate the way people say men shouldn't cry. Clifton has helped a lot.

I'll never accept the fact that my brother is gone, and I'm just so angry that it's happened. I want to be happy again, but I don't know when I will be. I think I will feel better when I go away to college. I know I'll work hard.

I will always wish that things were different. I guess that's what everyone wishes. I hope my parents will be more positive about things. I think that would help me to be more optimistic. I love my parents. I worry about them. I wish my father could be more open about his feelings so that it wouldn't hurt him so much.

Edward and Perry

✦

AGES 19 AND 15

Their sister Resa died at fifteen
of aplastic anemia, a blood-disorder disease.

Edward

Ever since I can remember, my sister was sick. She had diabetes as well as aplastic anemia, and she used to give herself insulin shots besides taking medicines for the anemia. She had to go into the hospital at various times during the last three years.

Even when she came home and seemed better, she knew she was going to die. She didn't come right out and say it until toward the end, when she'd break down and say, "I'm tired of being sick. I wish I would die." I didn't really understand and I'd scold her and we'd have fights. I felt really bad about that later.

About a week before she died, we had a little conference, which she initiated. She sat us all down and she said, "Family, I'm going to die." She wanted us to promise to go on and try to achieve our goals. We had to tell her right then and there how we felt about her dying. I told her, "You'll never be dead so long as I remember you."

Perry

I told her that I was going to miss her and stuff, that it wouldn't be the same without her. It was sad, wishing that it wasn't happening to her.

Edward

We all cried. She said, "I know there's a lot of things I don't understand about death, but I know I'm dying." She told us not to blame ourselves.

I was in the room with her when she died. I had to show a lot of strength afterward because everyone was breaking down. The worst part for me was the burial, seeing her get put into the ground.

Perry

Yeah, that was it. I felt I had to go because of my mother. I knew she was going to get hysterical again. Plus I think I owed it to my sister to be there.

We used to play together a lot. We would have play fights, and I'd call her names and stuff. I didn't really mean it, but I wish I hadn't done that. Sometimes when I'm playing I really miss my sister. I talk to my friend Tim about it. Resa liked him a lot.

One time we were at home and my ma was making us all clean up. And she called, "Resa, clean up the bathroom." Then she said, "Oh, I forgot," and she started crying. Sometimes Resa's old boyfriends would call and ask to speak to her. I would have to tell them she died. It was sad.

32

Edward

I'm further away from the shock now. Resa made me look on the bright side of things. To me her death was just physical, but her spirit—she's still here. She was such a good patient, she made such an effort in the hospital, and that made me say, "I have to get myself together for her and for me." I hurt, too, but I can't let that get me down. I have to keep striving the way she was always striving.

Michelle

✦

AGE 17

Her older brother committed suicide six months ago.

My parents, who are both musicians, were divorced two years ago, and my mother and I moved from Cleveland to New York. My brother was in college at the time. He was very sensitive, and he had a terrible temper, but he would never hurt anybody. Over the years my parents had sent him to psychiatrists, but he never stayed long with any of them. We knew he was mentally disturbed, but we didn't realize the seriousness of his illness until shortly before he died.

There had been an incident at school when he started throwing chairs around in his room at the dorm. The police came and took him to a mental hospital. After he was released, he went to see a doctor in New York, but when he returned to Cleveland, the school told him he couldn't stay.

I called him the day before he found out about school, to see how he was doing. He was very nervous and upset. He told a friend he had dinner with the next day, "My problems will be over soon." I think he just went into a gun shop and bought a gun.

My brother had said he would call me back the next night. When I didn't hear from him, I started to call but got no answer. At midnight the line was busy. Finally a policeman answered the phone. He said there had been an accident, that he couldn't tell me what was going on but that my father would call me. I was very nervous and was shaking, but I thought he was probably in the hospital. My mother thought he was dead.

About a half hour later my father called. I asked whether my brother was alive and my father said No. I don't think I'll ever forget that.

We didn't have a funeral. A few days after he died, I had a concert that I had to play. I'd won a competition to get to perform, so it was a big deal. That whole week I tried to put my brother's death out of my mind, and that was very hard, but I was able to do it. I thought that was the best thing to do. I didn't tell anyone except my boyfriend and my teacher. I think I should have told more people that week, but I wasn't ready to talk about it. Right after the concert there was a tremendous letdown, because then I had to face what had happened. Relatives were there, but no one congratulated me on the performance. It was strange. Some of them were probably mad at me for performing. I felt a little guilty, but my parents were supportive of my playing in the concert, so that was helpful.

The only thing I wish I had done at the time, though I couldn't because of the concert—I sort of wish I had seen my brother's body. I think maybe the shock of that, the realization that this body no longer had any life in it, would have helped. At the time I said, "No, I don't want to do that," but now I wish I had done it. Just to see him once and maybe to understand a little more.

I think one of the things that helped me most was holding up my mother. I thought I could handle the situation better than she could. I strengthened myself because I needed to be strong for her. It helped, too, having my boyfriend around, even though at the time I felt he wasn't helping me as much as he could. I know he tried very hard, and he was always there for me, but I wanted everything from him.

The person I spoke to most was myself, and then my boyfriend. I didn't really talk that much. At first I didn't cry much. My mom was always crying. I didn't want to cry in front of her because I wanted to show her that I would be OK. My mom thinks I didn't cry enough, but she's wrong, I think. I cried as much as I needed to.

I was depressed, and yes, I thought about suicide, but I knew I couldn't do it. My family really fell apart, and that's why I went to a doctor. My mom was in bad shape. I wanted to find a therapist who would offer some suggestions. A friend doesn't always know what to say or do if you're really feeling terrible. I think maybe you have to insist on being alone with the therapist, without your parents.

I think my father and I have adjusted quite well and go on with our everyday lives, but my mom hasn't. I think she feels very guilty. My relationship with my mother has gotten worse. When she devotes everything to me, it gets very difficult. I am constantly reminded I'm the only child left to my mother and father. I don't talk about my feelings anymore. Because my mother's having so much trouble, she thinks I'm hiding my feelings from her. She asks me these direct questions.

So few of my friends talk to me. I understand it's very difficult for people. They don't know what to say. I prefer it when they ask me about something a little bit on the outskirts, so there's a possibility I can get into it but I don't have to. The easiest way for me to start talking is when someone asks, "How's your mother? How's your father?"

I don't feel ashamed because my brother committed suicide. I know that society thinks it's a crime, that morally it is not accepted. I don't believe my friends think it's a bad mark for my family, but some people do think so. When people ask me about my brother, I don't tell them right away he committed suicide. I say other things, like he was very ill. I don't even like the expression, "commit suicide," although I use it. It sounds like a crime. "To take one's own life" sounds better.

I haven't had any nightmares, but I've had many dreams about my brother coming back to life. I was always there to stop him from hurting himself. I wish I had known what had been happening over the years. I wish I could have been more involved with him, but I was always so busy.

Six months after my brother's death I feel better. For a long time I slept a lot. I hardly practiced my violin. Slowly I realized I had to keep going. I feel very sad that my brother's gone, and I feel lonely that I'm not going to see him. Before, I thought that when someone dies in the family, it's the most horrible thing in the world and how could I continue. Now I feel much more optimistic in thinking about my own life and about doing things for myself. I'm going to be in college for the next four years, practicing very hard to be the best violinist I can be.

I don't really know what I can say that will help other people except that life really does go on for you. Though at the time nothing seems more important than your sibling's death, after a while you have to realize that your life is what's most important to you. It's going to be sad for a long time, but you will eventually be able to deal with it and get your life back in order.

Michelle is not her real name.

Tammy

◆

AGE 10

Her brother died of cancer of the brain at fourteen.

My brother Ronnie was fourteen when he died. He was sick for a long time. He had cancer.

Ronnie was like a father to me, not just a brother. He took care of me when Mom was at work. He cooked tomato soup. He fixed my hair. He was nice and he always helped me out. I just liked him.

When he got sick, it really hurt me a lot. I felt like I wasn't his sister as much because I was alone so often. I saw him in the hospital. I was happy to see him, but I felt bad when he was sick, throwing up and stuff. I didn't feel good. I think he was glad to see me. We talked.

I was at the Butlers' [friends of the family] house when he died. I said to Ms. Butler, "I have a feeling my brother is dead." She told me I was right, and I began to cry, but I couldn't believe it and still can't.

When my mom's crying, I tell her to stop crying, because it's the best thing. Ronnie is not in pain anymore. Sometimes she says that to me. Now and then she does get upset, but I don't want to cry anymore because it will take me weeks to get over it. I go to Ronnie's room and see his stuffed animals and his fish, and I don't feel so bad.

When I'm the most sad, I want to talk to my mom. Sometimes I ask her to come in my room, and I don't really tell her what I'm thinking because I'm afraid it might upset her. But I did tell her that I didn't think Ronnie was really in the coffin, that it didn't really look like him, and what if he's still alive? But I know it's not true, though it's hard to believe it.

It makes me mad at Mom when she cries. I know it's hurting Ronnie because he wouldn't like that. I try to pretend he's on a real long journey and that I'll see him one day. I know I will, but she makes me remember that I'm not going to see him for a long long while. She makes me upset.

School is OK. My teacher talked to me. He said I could leave the room whenever I needed to. But when I see my brother's friends, I feel bad. I start to cry. When I hear people talk about their brothers and how they hate them, it just makes me think, "Gee, I had a brother." We know we don't mean it. We say we hate them but we're really just mad. I wish I had a chance to tell him, "I love you. I will always love you."

I used to think about something happening to my mom when she went to the hospital. I wondered what would happen to me if she didn't come home. I said, "What if you got sick? What will happen to me? Will I be an orphan?" because all our relatives live in Germany. I'm not sure where my father is. I would like my mom to write a will so that I could know who would take care of me.

Maybe it is important to remember that if a brother or sister dies, they are not in pain anymore. Try not to feel sad, but cry if you have to.

Tammy wrote this story in the car when she and her mother went to the airport to pick up her grandmother before Ronnie's funeral.

42

Ron Swedberg

Died November 3, 1982

My brother died yesterday. I wish my brother didn't die.
He was so good to me. Me and my mom both love him
very much. He always stood up for me when my mom
yelled at me. I was lucky to have him as a brother. He
fought until God thought it was time for him to go to
heaven. I wish I was there when he died. Tomorrow I get
to see him and give him a kiss goodbye. But I will see him
when it's my turn to go to heaven. Ron's stuffed animals
miss him too. So does Fins, his fish. We all miss him. We
all love him.

Story by Tammy Swedberg
Sister of Ron Swedberg

Alecia

◆

AGE 17

*Her brother Barry and his best friend
were drowned when their homemade raft started
to break up and they tried to swim to shore.*

I was ten but I remember a lot. That Saturday, before Barry
went over to Dike's Lane—that's like a beach—I was sitting on
the porch, me and this girl Hope. Barry gave me a kiss and
said, "I'll see you later." That was all he said. And about three
hours later, we were playing ball with my two little cousins in
the backyard. This boy came up to me and said, "Lisa, Barry
went down in the water and he didn't come back up yet." My
mother heard it, and then the police came.

Barry's friend Pop had made a raft, and four of them went
out on it. They went too far out. Barry thought he could swim
to shore. "Jump, Mark. We'll swim," he said to his best friend.
The two who stayed on the raft were saved, but Barry and
Mark drowned.

The next few days were bad. We just kept crying. And my
father, he kept banging on the walls, yelling, "Oh, my son!" It
was really something to see.

I felt scared when I went to the wake, because it was my first time seeing somebody lying in the casket. I had a choice whether to go or not. My mother and I were walking in the door. I started crying and I turned back. Mom said, "Alecia, come see your brother for the last time." So I went to the casket. I asked her, "Can I kiss him?" She said I could, so I kissed him. I was sitting down afterwards when something happened and I started jumping and crying. It was just seeing my brother lying there, you know. It was like he was gone and I wouldn't ever see him again. That really took a hunk out of my heart.

We used to get up every night. My mother and my father would be sleeping in bed, and Barry, my other brother Michael and I used to get up at one in the morning and start roller-skating around the whole town. I had a lot of fun, roller-skating every night. I miss playing with him.

I've been dreaming about Barry a lot lately. My father too. [Alecia's father died two years ago.] I think that when I wake up in the morning, they'll be there.

I try to help my mom a lot. I try to do good in school for her, and when she tells me a certain time to be in the house, I try to come in. I tell her, "Don't cry," or I wipe her face. I just let her cry but I try not to. Mom tells me that it's going to hurt but you have to live on. When somebody dies, you have to keep on living.

Debbie

♦

AGE 14

Her brother Anthony died of leukemia at seventeen.

Anthony had lived with leukemia for two years. Leukemia is the medical term for a disease in which there is uncontrollable multiplication of white blood cells. He'd just gotten over a relapse when he developed appendicitis. Because of Anthony's leukemia, the doctor wasn't sure if he should operate on Anthony's appendix, but he did and the operation was a success. The day Anthony came out of surgery, he got chicken pox and had a very high fever, which made him have convulsions. He couldn't walk and he could hardly talk. He lost his mind.

I couldn't understand how the doctors could have let all these terrible things happen to Anthony. I was blaming the whole world when it wasn't anybody's fault. I was always home worrying about myself and being selfish instead of being worried about my only brother.

I knew he was going to die, but I never thought it would happen soon, and I didn't take advantage of the little time I had left with him. I think I should have gone to see him. Maybe it

49

would have made me feel a little better, but I just didn't want to remember him like that. I was afraid to see him looking the way he did.

I started to feel uncomfortable around people because they were always feeling sorry for me. I didn't need anyone's sympathy or pity. All I needed was to be alone.

Anthony was getting weaker day by day, and he started having problems breathing. One day my mother told me Anthony was going to come home for a visit. I tried to change her mind by telling her he probably wouldn't know where he was or what was going on, but she told me that she wanted me to be home when he came. I didn't know how I was going to react to Anthony, and I just didn't think I could handle it. I was so relieved when she said I didn't have to be there.

The day of Anthony's visit, I went to my friend's house. I didn't tell anyone about his visit. When I got home, I found a letter from Anthony, and it said:

Dear Debbie:
I waited for you for an hour and a half but I had to leave.
I love you.

Love,
Anthony

When some of my friends heard that I wasn't home to see him, they started to yell at me. The last thing I needed was my friends telling me how wrong I was. After a while people started to see my point of view and realized what I was going through. If only they knew what I felt when I saw him in the hospital room in pain and suffering so much.

I didn't want to worry my parents about me. They already had Anthony to worry about, and they didn't need my problems. I felt I was a burden to them, and I started to get jealous of Anthony since he was getting so much of my mother's attention and I wasn't.

Now that I think about it, I realize that I should have spent

more time with my brother, but I didn't want to face the fact that Anthony was going to die.

On Thursday, October 14, I came home from school. My mother was supposed to go with me to a meeting about Catholic high schools that evening, but she wasn't home and I was so angry. Finally she called and she told me Anthony was probably going to die that night. When she told me that, I didn't know what to say. No words would come out of my mouth. I knew she was crying. About a half hour later Anthony's social worker called and said he had died a few minutes earlier. I just stood in shock. When my mother came home, she talked to me and started to tell me that it was for the best. That night I cried like I never cried before.

I didn't go to the funeral. I decided to stay at my uncle's house. I didn't want to remember Anthony like that. I wanted to remember him laughing and always joking around. My family understood how I felt, and they didn't try to talk me into going.

At school I can talk to the guidance counselor. He's a priest, and he and Anthony were close, so whenever I want to talk about him, I just go down to the counselor's office. He helps me understand what's happening at home. Now I know when my parents feel protective, it's because of Anthony. He always tells me to try and talk things out with them.

I had this assignment in school to write a story, and I wrote about Anthony. It was called "The Last Days." It was as if I got everything off my chest, put everything I was thinking into words. My teacher and my friends thought it was good, and they were proud of me for writing it because it was hard to do.

My family has been very good to me. I've learned to accept the fact that Anthony isn't with us anymore. I'm glad he isn't suffering.

The Norton Anthology
of Modern Poetry

Edited by
Richard Ellmann and Rob...

Sheila

◆

AGE 19

Her younger sister Jennifer,
age twelve, was hit by a motorcycle
when she was playing flashlight tag.

I was a freshman in high school when Jennifer died. It was spring vacation, just after Easter. I'd been to the movies with some friends, and when I got home, my grandmother's car was outside. I thought it was odd. I walked into the kitchen and everyone was waiting for me. My mother was crying and she looked at me and she said, "It's our Jen. She's dead." My initial reaction was bad. Everyone stepped forward to hug me, but I felt almost nauseous. I just wanted them to get away from me.

I wasn't given many details of the accident. I never really asked. Some people find it important to know everything, but it never occurred to me. I know that Jennifer was spending the night over at her friend Sandy's. Sandy's family lives in a little dead-end street off a busy road. I guess the kids were all playing flashlight tag and decided to cross onto the busy road. A motorcycle came around the bend and hit her.

Jennifer and I shared a room. I think we had a special relationship because of sharing. If she got yelled at in school, and she was thinking about it at night and started to cry, I'd be there. She used to get into my bed at night sometimes.

We fought too. She always used to take her underwear off and leave it on my bed, and that used to make me mad.

After the accident I used to dream she was alive. Then I'd wake up and see her bed in my room, unslept in. My room is changed now. For a while I wouldn't change it. I didn't want to put her in a box in the attic—that's what it felt like. I've kept some special things, like her Snoopy doll.

I never saw her body, which now I think was a mistake. At the time, though, I thought it was right. I think now that seeing the body is important, not in a morbid sense but because there is a peace that comes from seeing a body, knowing that the life isn't there. It took me longer to accept because I didn't see her body.

I didn't go to the burial. It scared me, all of a sudden. I went back to the house after the funeral with a friend of the family and my friend Greg. Greg and I went to kindergarten together, and he lives down the street. He was a very important shoulder for me to cry on, and he didn't give stupid answers to all the questions like "Why did this terrible thing happen? Why Jennifer and not me?"

I was fifteen when Jennifer died, and it was my first year in high school. That's a time of transition in your life. You're growing up, you're learning things socially. Those years are both painful and happy, and having to cope with something like the death of a sister can be overwhelming.

A lot of my teachers took into consideration what was going on with me at home. A guidance counselor called me to her office a few times, to see how I was adjusting. I found that disruptive because I'd come out of class and she'd talk to me about it and I'd cry. I'd have to go back to the class all puffy-eyed, and the eyes that were already looking at me looked even more—"Ooh, she's crying."

There were some special teachers. I'll never forget one time when I was a sophomore and we had to see a movie. It was one of those days when everything went wrong. I came in late, I dropped all my books and then there was a pop quiz in one class, so when I finally got to Religion, I thought, "Oh, good, a movie. I can just sit at the back of this class and veg out." But the teacher showed this movie and he hadn't told anyone ahead of time what it was about. It was about a girl who was hit by a car, and it presented the other side, the viewpoint of the guy who hit her and what he was going through. Up to this point I was so angry at the guy who hit Jennifer, but I feel so sorry for him now. I don't know if I could live knowing that I killed somebody.

But this wasn't just something you could take and go on to the next class. I was hysterical. I was sitting at the back of the room sobbing, and I was angry. The teacher came up to me and he said, "I'm so sorry. I should have prepared you and I didn't." And he sat with me while I cried, and he held me and talked to me. There were two classes he should have been teaching, but he had someone cover for him. When I got home from school that day, he called to see how I was. So there were special people around who would help.

I can remember the first Christmas after her death. I was so angry. I can remember sitting at the dinner table and feeling I was the only one recognizing that she wasn't there. I'm sure everybody else was in as much pain as I was, but no one said anything. I drew a portrait of her and gave it to my parents on Christmas Eve, so in my own way I made sure she was recognized. You know, grief is so selfish. You always see what you're feeling, and it's hard to see beyond what you're feeling into what someone else is going through, especially when you're grieving over the same person. You have your own special relationship with that person. My relationship with Jennifer was different from mine with my other sister or with my mother. I can't say it was closer, but she was different and special to me and unique in her own way.

The past two years I've been at school on her birthday, and I've had a mass said. This year it was a priest I'd never met before who said the mass, and I talked to him beforehand. He was just wonderful. He mentioned her name, he said, "This mass is being offered for Jennifer." He treated it so well that it was a really good experience. I felt close to her and to my parents. I went back and called my parents just to tell them what I was thinking about.

Some days I'll think of something funny that she used to do, but I get upset when people's younger brothers and sisters come up to visit. Just two weeks ago I was walking down the hall and I saw somebody come in with their younger brother who was obviously up for the weekend. He was a young high-school student and he had that "Wow, college!" look in his eyes. As I walked upstairs, I was just full of rage at how unfair it was. God, I wanted to share that with Jennifer. There are things that can never be brought back. I never got to drive her around when I got my license—things like that.

One time my father found a poem that I'd written about Jennifer when I was in high school. He had tears in his eyes and that blew my mind. It was a good moment. We were close, we had both loved Jennifer, and we were sad.

Visitation Rites

I

On the swing
  I am pushing—
You are flying,
  Screeching laughter,
  breathless laughter.
Hot beach sun
  bakes, my cinnamon chest
cooled suddenly as
you swoop backward
  breezing past me.
"Watch me, I can jump!"
"No, don't . . ."
  Too late.
Hot, salty tears and
salty, wet hair
  against my shoulder.

II

I sit up.
  In the dark of the night
sleep flies from my body—
  I look over and
I see your bed.
  Empty, cold,
like the tomb you
  sleep in now.

Chris

✦

AGE 18

His brother Blair, age two and a half, was drowned.

My tragedy happened four years ago. I had a very young brother who was two and a half, my only brother. My mom divorced when I was about two. When I was about five, I used to say, "Mom, when are you going to get married again, so I can get a brother? I want a brother." I went fatherless from two until seven, and then my mom got married. I was in sixth grade when my brother was born. He was my half brother, but he was my brother to me, just like my stepdad's my father.

I was so happy to have a brother. My mom told me she was pregnant before she told my dad, because it was right around his birthday, and she kind of wanted that to be his present. I woke up one morning and there was this note, "Going up to the hospital." I went to school and then I was called to the principal's office. There was my dad, and he looked at me and he said, "How do you feel about having a brother?" They named him Blair, a combination of their two names Bob and Claire, and I was so happy to have him.

I used to take care of him all the time, too. I always played with him and tried to get him to do things. For such a young kid, he had an incredible personality, and he was really good with his hands. He was constantly getting into mischief. My grandfather drove down to the end of the street and left my brother in the car with the car keys on the seat. Blair picked up the car keys, and out of five keys he figured out which one went into the ignition.

He had so much personality. He couldn't really verbalize that well, but he'd come into my room when I was asleep, and he'd wake me up and look around my room and say, "Gee, what a mess." Most little kids, they have their toys and they don't put them away, but he put everything back in its spot. There were lots of things that I saw in myself that I didn't like and I didn't want him to pick up. I wanted him to have the characteristics that I did like in myself, like my openness and affection. I was more of a parent than a brother to him.

I had just turned fourteen when he died. I was fourteen on June 2 and he died July 24. He would have been three in October. We were staying at a house belonging to some friends, and there was a pool in the backyard. I'd been playing with him, and I had to go to the bathroom. When I came back, my mother said, "Chris, go look for Blair. I don't see him." There was a puppy barking by the poolside. When I got a little closer, I saw him and I jumped in. I was screaming. My mother and father came out. We went through fifteen hours of seeing him in the hospital, with tubes and everything. Finally he died.

I had a very hard year. I was scared. My friends really didn't know how to treat me. I was suicidal and writing notes and stuff. Finally my parents sent me to a psychiatrist, and I got two years of counseling.

The one thing I want to say is that nothing is that bad that you can't live through it. To take your own life because of something like that is incredibly stupid, because you'll find that life is very beautiful and there's a lot out there to find and to look forward to. When it comes to dealing with your loss, seek help. It doesn't mean you're weak. It doesn't mean that you can't help yourself, because you just need help. You need a starting point. Counseling isn't for everybody but give it a try.

If you want to start a group like I finally did, get enough people your age interested and maybe one adult and let them say what they've been through. To know you're not alone is so comforting, because some of the feelings make me feel so isolated, like "O my God, am I crazy?" You know, some of the feelings are so out of nowhere. "Where are they coming from? Is there something wrong with me?" It's important to know you're not the only one feeling that.

Kim

◆

AGE 21

Her brother Joseph died of Cooley's anemia.

My brother Joseph died four years ago, when he was nineteen. He had Cooley's Anemia, a hereditary blood disease. I have the disease too. We were born normal but as we grew, our bone marrow didn't develop certain cells, so we had to have blood transfusions. You can get an iron overload from the transfusions, and this means your heart has to work harder. Joseph had a lot of heart problems.

We were very close because we had blood transfusions together, at the same hospital. Joseph was very good to me. As a small child, I couldn't understand why I had to go to the hospital, and he would tell me, "You have to do this." When we were growing up, no one told us we had a disease we were going to have for the rest of our lives. Joseph explained it to me when I was about eight years old. He helped me in so many ways to cope with what I have. We were never without each other.

No one told me Joseph wasn't going to make it. He was in the hospital for twelve days. He wasn't responding to medication, and as the days passed, I saw he was getting weaker and weaker.

I asked people what was happening to my brother, and they wouldn't tell me. They said I was too young to know. I said, "What do you mean? I'm his sister."

I couldn't bear to see him anymore. Every time I saw him I would cry. I guess because of that he told me he wasn't going to die, but I think he knew.

My father called me at work and told me not to go to the hospital, so I went home. My mom was crying and I knew Joseph had died. I sat down on the couch and started crying, but I couldn't let it all out. I went in my room and I cried and cried. My father came in. He told me it was all right to cry.

My parents tried to comfort me, but they were in such grief themselves. I didn't have such a close relationship with my sisters, but they helped a little. It was really just me and my parents. I saw that my parents were handling it better than I was, maybe because they were concerned that I would break down more if I saw them cry more.

There was a two-day wake and then the funeral. Doctors and people from the hospital came to the wake. One doctor told me I shouldn't go to the wake, but I didn't like him so I was determined that he wasn't going to tell me what to do. I went out of respect—and a little bit out of spite.

I think a wake is horrible. It puts the family through more grief. I regret going to the wake because now I have this image of my brother, a mental image of him in the coffin. I have to think hard before I can think of him as a person and of the good times we had. Some people might be able to hack it, but I couldn't.

I have a picture of my brother when he was about six and I was four, and we have our arms around each other. Other than that, I don't have anything of his. In the Chinese tradition, when you bury someone, you bury his stuff with him, so that you also bury the pain. When Joseph was buried, he wore his graduation suit; his graduation ring and trophy, and his graduation certificate, his radio and his tapes were all buried with him.

After the funeral I changed hospitals and things started getting better for me. Now the doctors tell me what is going to happen with tests, and they are optimistic about me. I still have to have transfusions every four weeks. I feel fine but I can't overexert myself.

I have one good friend, Ann, who knows about my disease. We got closer after my mother died two years ago. She is very supportive. Most of the time she doesn't say anything, but knowing that she listens helps me. It is more comfortable talking to her than to a professional like a psychologist or a psychiatrist.

It's still painful talking about my brother, but now I can do it. The pain will always be there, but I've come to understand that this is the way it is going to be and I've learned to cope with it. Now I have a totally different view of life. I take it more seriously, and I try to accomplish as much as I can. Time has helped me most of all.

Kim is not her real name. At her request there is no photograph.

Lisa

◆

AGE 18

Four years ago, her sister Sandy
was murdered by a man the family did not know.

A man telephoned one afternoon and said his name was Dr. Roberts. He told me he was looking for a baby-sitter, so I woke up Sandy to tell her about the call. The man told her he would meet her and then they would walk back to his house.

By six o'clock my mom was getting worried. She looked up the man in the telephone book, but there was no one with the name and address he had given us. My parents got very worried, and my dad went to every house in the area. I remember staying up until two in the morning and telling myself that nothing was wrong, nothing had happened. I didn't want to imagine anything bad happening.

The police came the next day. The first thing I heard was my dad screaming. They had found Sandy's body and the man who killed her. My first reaction was that I wanted to kill the man who did it. I was hysterical.

Everybody told me, "Lisa, you have to be strong for your parents," and "You must be quiet because you'll make your mother upset." I worked hard not to cry. I felt I had to keep my feelings to myself, and that's what I did. Everyone told me to put my feelings aside, like my feelings weren't as important as my parents'. I wish someone had asked me how I felt, maybe not even to talk about it but just to let me cry. I think it would have helped. I wanted someone to bring up the question of my feelings with me. No one did. I never cried until about a year later, when it suddenly hit me that she wasn't around.

I remember at first I felt very guilty. My dad felt guilty so I thought maybe I should too. I felt guilty because I answered the phone and woke Sandy up about the baby-sitting job. But I realize now there was no way I could have known what would happen.

I did very badly in school that year. I didn't care about anything. I was cutting classes. I started getting into drugs, but then I realized that wasn't helping. In fact, it made things worse because it was hurting my parents, too. They were going through a hard time, and then I just made it harder for them.

I'm doing better in school now, though I'm still not sure how new people I meet will treat me after they know about what happened to my sister. I think I've changed a lot in the last few years. I want to do something that will make my parents proud of me. My grades have improved, and I'm not getting into trouble the way I used to. I've done it all by myself.

I think parents can help their children by telling them, "I'm always here if you need me." It's important for them just to be there when their children are ready to talk.

Just recently I was talking with my dad about my younger sister not being able to speak about Sandy. It's been four years now, and she still can't even say Sandy's name. I'd like to talk to her about it. I think if she would talk about Sandy's death, she would feel better, but it's probably her way of handling it.

At first I had mixed feelings about being interviewed for this book, but then I thought maybe I can help someone. I think it might have helped me. Maybe someone who feels it's very hard to talk to anyone will read this book and it will help them to open up and not feel so alone.

Sharon

✦

AGE 18

Her brother Stanley, age 10, died of a brain tumor.

My mother told me Stanley was sick, but I didn't think he was
going to die. I thought he was just in the hospital for his regular
checkup, but then they told me that he had a tumor in his head
and that he couldn't see.

When I was told my brother had died, I just left the room. I
couldn't even cry. My father cried. He never cried in his life,
but he started crying. Because I couldn't cry I began to wonder
if there was something wrong with me. Did I really love my
brother? When I talked to my mother about it, she said, "Well,
we all handle situations in different ways."

Eventually I did break down. I was talking to my mother one
night and we began reminiscing about my brother's sickness.
She said something about the big needles he used to have in his
back for a spinal tap, and I started thinking about him suffering. I told her that if it ever happened to me, I couldn't take the
pain. And tears started coming out of my eyes. I missed him. I

let it all out and I felt better afterwards. I thought I was OK but now I realize I was hurting. I was hurting a lot.

After Stanley died, my mother had another baby. Someone told us the baby would replace my brother, but that's ridiculous. No one could. However, now my sister is growing up, she's exactly like him. She acts like him, she even looks like him. But I treat her as herself, Tamika, not like my brother.

Not a day goes by without my thinking about him. We had a lot of fun. We were really close and we did everything together. I could talk to him when I had a problem, even though he was a young kid. I used to beat him up sometimes, and I don't take that back because he deserved it, but I wish I could have told him more often that I loved him.

After he died, I really got into studying. I want to be a doctor, so maybe I can help someone else. My brother said I would be a good doctor, so I want to try.

Karen

♦

AGE 24

*Her brother was killed
at nineteen when his car crashed.*

My brother was killed in a car accident two years ago, in September. His name was Billy and he was nineteen at the time. We don't really understand what happened as far as the accident goes. He was all alone in the car, and I guess it was about twelve o'clock at night. He hit a pole, and there were no witnesses and no other cars involved. So we're not really quite sure what happened.

I got a call about three o'clock in the morning from my mother. She called from the hospital. Initially I thought maybe he'd just broken his arm, or something like that. You never think the worst. As I got closer to the hospital, I started realizing that my mother wouldn't call me at three o'clock in the morning if my brother broke his arm. I worked my way up from this casual "he probably broke his arm" to "he's probably dead." I had gotten myself into a frenzy by the time I reached the hospital. All of the nurses were standing at the front door waiting for me, and they said, "Are you Billy's sister?" As soon as I got into the waiting room and I saw my parents, I knew that he was either dead or not going to live very long, because they were bouncing off the walls. I walked in, and my mother sat me down and she said, "I don't really know how to say this to you." And I knew what she was going to say, and I interrupted her and I said, "Please, just don't say it. I know what you're going to tell me, and I'm really sorry, whatever happened"—which later struck me as funny, that I was saying I was sorry to my mother that my brother died, really taking myself out of this scene, like I was a bystander.

I remember we started to leave the hospital once, I guess about five o'clock. And we couldn't go. We walked down the hall about halfway, and I said, "I just can't leave." Before I got there, before I walked into the hospital, he was alive. Walking out of the hospital and him not coming with us meant he was dead. I just didn't want to accept that we were going and leaving him behind.

Finally we had to go. We went back to the house and we just sat in the living room. I kept looking at the door, expecting him to come in and say, "Ha ha, it's all a joke." Or wake up—I thought this was a nightmare and I was going to wake up.

Then we did all the other things. We went to the funeral parlor. We checked out the flowers. Then we drove into Queens to tell my grandparents. My mother kept saying, "If she wants to be with us, then she should be with us," but I think my father wanted to protect me from all of this. He didn't want me to have to go through this scene that he knew there would be at my grandmother's house or at the funeral parlor or at the florist. He was trying to be sensitive to me, but I'm really glad that I chose to do what I wanted to do, which was to do all these little errands with them, because I think I needed to feel the pain. I don't think you get better until you've been at the lowest that you can be.

My parents and I have become very close. I think we realized that we spent too much time doing our own little thing, not really paying attention to each other, not really communicating with each other. My parents are much closer to each other than they were before. They spend a lot more time together. And they're a lot more sensitive to each other's needs and feelings.

I'm so envious of all these other kids who've got other brothers and sisters. I feel very cheated. I lost my brother Billy. But I also lost a whole relationship. I will never have that again. There's no chance that I am ever going to have another brother or sister. Once upon a time we were four people, and we went all these places together and we were a family. We've got pictures of four people by the Christmas tree. Some day there'll be just me.

I don't know if this is something that all surviving kids feel, but I have this very strong desire to make it better for my mother and father, to make it easy as possible for them to live through this.

When it first happened, I had to talk about it a lot. I think that the longer a person is dead, the more personal the whole situation becomes. I think you individualize your own grief. And as much as my family still share things together, a lot of what I feel I want to keep inside now, and I want it to be between me and Billy, and I don't necessarily want to express it to my mother or anyone else. And she feels the same way. I think it's the final stage of adjusting. It's how I deal with it, inside me, which is going to get me through this.

When people ask me if I have brothers or sisters, I find that there isn't any way I can deny Billy's existence. Depending on how I feel at the time, how well I know the person that I'm talking to and how I think this person is going to react to what I want to say, I will either say, "Yes, I have a brother," and wait to be asked what my brother is doing and then say that he's dead, or I will just come clean and say, "My brother died in a car accident two years ago."

Some kids deny that they had a brother or sister. I think it's OK to feel that way because you're really only protecting yourself. You're not saying you don't love this person and this person never was here; you're just putting up a little wall because you don't want to be hurt at that moment.

You know, someone can say, "I understand you're feeling very bad," and that's OK. Or they might say, "I understand how difficult this must be for you." But for someone to say, "Oh, yes, I know exactly how you feel," seems ridiculous to me. I don't want to force them to try and understand. They just can't, and that's all right.

I belong to a sibling group that is an extension of a parent group called The Compassionate Friends. We meet once a month and we talk about our experiences, how our brother or sister died, what our relationship was with that person before and how we're dealing with what's going on now. There are usually about ten people who attend the meetings on a regular basis, and the age range varies.

There are kids who come once and don't come back, because it's not for them. There are kids who come and don't talk but just listen—that's not to say they're not getting anything out of it, but they just want to sit and listen. And there are other kids who do a lot of talking and have worked through a lot of problems in this group. I think it's helpful to everyone, not just people who don't have any other surviving brothers and sisters. It is sometimes even better to talk to strangers about your feelings.

Even though people have the same type of loss, there are so many different reactions and so many different ways that people deal with it. All of it is good. I mean, all of it is OK if it's what makes you comfortable. There's no way you can really say to a person, "You should do this," or "You should do that." The only thing you might tell a person to do is to try to be honest and to try not to run away from their feelings and themselves.

Acknowledgments

✦

Many thanks to:

The families who worked with me on this project.

The Compassionate Friends, Connecticut Chapter
Suzanne Van Vechten for introducing me to the families in her area and for her interest in and enthusiasm for the project.

Charles "Mo" Moroney and Charlene Spicer for printing the photos. Mo's involvement is especially appreciated since he and his wife Rita lost their daughter Kathy this past year.

Refna Wilkin, my editor, for her persistent encouragement, patience, sensitive editorial advice and talent for pulling it all together.

My friends—Ann Zalesky, Mort Herskowitz, Maryann DeLeo, Marc Wallace, Rudy Garcia.

And as ever Bernard W. Scholz.

✦

The Compassionate Friends is an organization for bereaved parents with more than three hundred chapters in the United

States and abroad. Many of the chapters have teen or sibling groups. For more information, write to:

The Compassionate Friends, Inc.
National Headquarters
P.O. Box 3969
Oak Brook
Illinois 60522-3696